Jacques Cartier

Andrew Santella

Heinemann Library
Chicago, Illinois

© 2002 Reed Educational & Professional Publishing
Published by Heinemann Library,
an imprint of Reed Educational & Professional Publishing,
Chicago, Illinois

Customer Service 888-454-2279

Visit our website at www.heinemannlibrary.com

Design and maps by Wilkinson Design
Printed and bound in the U.S.A. by Lake Book Manufacturing, Inc.

06 05 04 03 02
10 9 8 7 6 5 4 3 2 1

Library of Congress Cataloging-in-Publication Data
Santella, Andrew.
        Jacques Cartier / Andrew Santella.
              p. cm. — (Groundbreakers)
        Includes bibliographical references and index.
        Summary: Presents an account of Cartier's life and explorations and
        examines their impact on history and the world.
              ISBN 1-58810-594-6
              1. Cartier, Jacques, 1491-1557—Juvenile literature. 2.
        Explorers—America—Biography—Juvenile literature. 3.
        Explorers—France—Biography—Juvenile literature. 4.
        Canada—History—To 1763 (New France)—Juvenile literature. [1. Cartier,
        Jacques 1491-1557. 2. Explorers. 3. Canada—Discovery and exploration.
        4. Canada—History—To 1763 (New France)] I. Title. II. Series.
              E133.C3 S26 2001
              971.01'13'092—dc21

                                        2001004030

Acknowledgments
The author and publishers are grateful to the following for permission to reproduce copyright material:
pp. 4, 8, 10, 14, 17, 18, 23, 25, 40 The Granger Collection, New York; pp. 5, 6 Hubert Stadler/Corbis; pp. 7, 20 Corbis; p. 9 Historical Picture Archive/Corbis; pp. 11, 36 Wolfgang Kaehler/Corbis; p. 12 Academy of Natural Sciences of Philadelphia/Corbis; p. 13 W. A. Montevecchi; p. 15 Austrian Archives/Corbis; pp. 16, 21, 28, 30, 33, 35 North Wind Picture Archives; pp. 19, 31 Hulton/Archive by Getty Images; p. 22 Ron Watts/Corbis; p. 24 Lee Snider/Corbis; p. 26 Stock Montage; p. 27 Gunter Marx Photography/Corbis; p. 29 Biophoto Associates/Photo Researchers, Inc.; pp. 32, 38 Bettman/Corbis; p. 34 Richard A. Cooke/Corbis; p. 37 Jose Manuel Sanchis Calvete/Corbis; p. 39 John Heseltine/Corbis; p. 41 Paul A. Souders/ Corbis.

Cover photograph courtesy of The Granger Collection, New York.

Every effort has been made to contact copyright holders of any material reproduced in this book. Any omissions will be rectified in subsequent printings if notice is given to the publisher.

Some words are shown in bold, **like this.** You can find out what they mean by looking in the glossary.

Contents

Today, many of the people who live in the large Canadian cities of Montréal and Québec speak French. The street signs there are in French, and most of the rivers and mountains have French names. Jacques Cartier, a sea captain and explorer who lived 500 years ago, is partly responsible for this.

Discovering the St. Lawrence River

At a time when European explorers were still mapping the coastlines of North and South America, Cartier plunged deep into the interior of the continent. He sailed three times from France to explore what is now called Canada. He claimed the land he found there for the king of France. Those claims became the foundation for centuries of French influence along the St. Lawrence River.

Jacques Cartier traveled as far west as the site of modern-day Montréal, and his influence is still felt today.

Cartier explored the St. Lawrence River, one of the mightiest waterways in the entire continent. He was the first European to sail up the river, into the green and wooded valley that would one day be populated by French settlers. He visited the future sites of Québec and Montréal. When Cartier arrived there, he found villages occupied by the Iroquois. One day, the descendants of those Native Americans would be replaced by the French settlers who followed in Cartier's footsteps.

French is still spoken in many parts of Canada, including Montréal, shown in this photograph.

Cartier's search

Cartier came to North America for several reasons. Like other European explorers, he was looking for the **Northwest Passage**—a shortcut from Europe to Asia that would lead around or through the Americas. If such a passage could be found, it would be much easier for Europeans to get the spices and other products they desired from Asia. Cartier also hoped he would find gold to bring back to France. Finally, on his last trip, he attempted to establish a French **colony** on the St. Lawrence River.

Cartier failed to find gold and he failed to find the Northwest Passage. His attempt at building a colony was a failure, too. However, Cartier's explorations laid the groundwork for a great French **empire** in Canada.

THE NORTHWEST PASSAGE

In 1522, a voyage led by Ferdinand Magellan returned to Spain after sailing around the world. The voyage had taken three years and Magellan died along the way. Magellan's crew had to sail around the dangerous southern tips of South America and Africa, but explorers from other European nations hoped to find a shorter route to Asia. Many hoped to find a water route through the northern reaches of North America—the Northwest Passage. The search for such a passage kept explorers busy for hundreds of years. Only in the 20th century, with powerful ice-breaking ships, were sailors able to travel from the Atlantic Ocean to the Pacific Ocean by sailing north of North America.

The Age of Exploration

Jacques Cartier was born in 1491 in the French port city of St. Malo. His birth came at the very beginning of a new age of European exploration. In the years following his birth, explorers from all the great nations of Europe headed west across the Atlantic Ocean to explore the "New World" of the Americas.

Exploring the Americas

Just one year after Cartier's birth, Christopher Columbus sailed west, looking for Asia, and found the Americas blocking his way. In 1497, England sent John Cabot across the ocean to explore the icy waters on the shore of present-day Newfoundland. Cabot returned without the spices of Asia, and without the gold that some hoped to find in the Americas. However, he did make one discovery that interested the people of St. Malo. Cabot found one of the greatest fishing spots in the world.

St. Malo lies on the Gulf of St. Malo, an arm of the Atlantic Ocean.

St. Malo

The town of St. Malo is on the northern coast of France. Many of the people of St. Malo made their living from the sea. They piloted ocean-going ships and sank their nets into the sea to catch loads of fish. In fact, St. Malo was known throughout France for her skilled sailors and hardy fishermen.

Fishing the Grand Banks

The fishermen were naturally eager to learn more about the fishing ground that Cabot found. It was called the Grand Banks, and it was located off the coast of Newfoundland. The waters there were brimming with cod. To the people of St. Malo, this humble fish was almost as good as gold.

John Cabot was born in the Italian city of Genoa, but he sailed for England.

Fish was an important food for the Catholic countries of Europe, and a fortune could be made supplying fish. Very quickly, the fishermen of St. Malo began to sail west to fish the waters off the Newfoundland coast. It was on fishing trips such as these that young Jacques Cartier probably learned to sail.

LOST EXPLORER

John Cabot sailed under the flag of England, but he was born in Italy in 1461 as Giovanni Caboto. As a young man, he moved to Bristol, an English seaport. From there, he led voyages to North America. He discovered Newfoundland in 1497. The following year, he left England for another trip to Newfoundland, but he was never seen again. His son, Sebastian, was also an important explorer.

Sailing for the King

No one knows Cartier's exact date of birth. Nor does anyone know exactly how he lived the first 42 years of his life. However, records kept by churches and town officials do tell us some things about Cartier. For example, we know that Cartier married the daughter of a local official in 1519. Historians also use clues to help make guesses about Cartier's life. For example, we know that Cartier spoke Portuguese. Based on this information, historians think that he probably learned the language on Portuguese ships, from Portuguese sailors. This means that Cartier may have sailed to the Portuguese colonies in Brazil when he was a young man.

Giovanni da Verrazano explored from North Carolina to Newfoundland.

Orders from the king

By the time he was 42 years old, Cartier must have been one of the most respected sailors and **navigators** in France. One document calls him "master pilot of the port of Saint-Malo." In 1533, Cartier entered the pages of history. Francis I, king of France, chose Cartier to lead a voyage across the Atlantic Ocean. His mission was to find the mysterious **Northwest Passage.** The king instructed Cartier to sail for Newfoundland and to explore the waters of the region. The orders were dated October 31, 1533.

Danger at sea

It had been 36 years since John Cabot had disappeared searching for a Northwest Passage near Newfoundland. Since then, several Spanish and Portuguese explorers had joined the search. None succeeded. Fishing boats regularly worked the Grand Banks, but the waters beyond remained a mystery. Many sailors feared the icy and foggy seas along the North American shoreline.

Cartier was not the first French sailor to explore the waters of North America. King Francis had sent an Italian navigator named Giovanni da Verrazano west in 1524. Like Cartier, he was looking for a Northwest Passage. Verrazano sailed up and down 1,000 miles (1,600 kilometers) of shoreline, but he found no way to Asia. Some historians believe that Cartier may have sailed with Verrazano, but no one is sure. By 1534, Cartier was ready to lead his own voyage.

King Francis I sent Cartier to explore the waters near Newfoundland.

THE RACE FOR RICHES

The nations of Europe competed with each other to find and explore new lands. Each king hoped his explorers would return from the Americas with riches. Spain grew wealthy from gold and silver they found in Central America and South America. King Francis I of France knew that Spanish explorers were helping make Spain rich. He hoped that explorers like Cartier might find their own supplies of gold and silver in North America.

An Ocean Crossing

YOU CAN FOLLOW JACQUES CARTIER'S JOURNEY ON THE MAPS ON PP. 42-43.

Cartier's first task was to select the ships and the sailors he would lead to North America. He did not receive much help from the town leaders of St. Malo. They thought the journey Cartier planned was too risky, and they refused to give him the supplies and the sailors he needed. Finally, Cartier had to appeal to the king, Francis I, who declared that no ships could leave St. Malo until Cartier received the help he needed. That solved the problem. Cartier chose two wooden ships, each capable of carrying 60 tons. They were typical ships of the time, with two or three **masts** that held up square sails. Cartier stocked the ships with enough supplies to last from April until September.

Ships of Cartier's time were built for carrying cargo, not passengers. Long ocean crossings could be very uncomfortable.

On April 20, 1534, Cartier and his crew left St. Malo. The stiff springtime winds that blow from east to west across the Atlantic Ocean meant that Cartier was sailing at an ideal time of year. With the wind at their backs, he and his ships covered more than 2,000 miles (3,200 kilometers) in 20 days. That may sound like a long time in this age of air travel, but in Cartier's time that was a very fast ocean crossing. Christopher Columbus's first voyage in 1492 had taken more than three times that long.

10

Before accurate sea-going clocks were invented, sailors kept track of time by using a sandglass, or hourglass. The glass was divided in two compartments, with one of the compartments filled with sand. It took exactly an hour for the sand from one compartment to drip into the other compartment. It was the job of the ship's boy to turn the hourglass over as soon as all the sand filled one compartment.

Life on board

Cartier's trip was quick, but like all ocean crossings of that time, it was difficult. The ships of Cartier's time were not comfortable places for sailors. They slept crowded together, on flimsy mats or on **hammocks.** They ate hard biscuits that over time grew moldy and became filled with **maggots.** The salt water of the ocean was not fit for drinking, so they had to dip into barrels of drinking water that often had a thin film of scum floating on the top. The ships themselves were often filled with mice, roaches, and even rats. The only way to keep these creatures under control was to carry a few cats on board.

After three weeks in these conditions, Cartier's sailors must have been glad to see land. However, when they did sight land, they found their path blocked. Cartier had made it across the ocean so quickly that the ice floating in the North Atlantic had not yet melted for the spring. Finding ice blocking his way, Cartier had to wait ten days for it to melt. Only then could his ships sail on safely.

Cartier found ice blocking his path when he reached the shore of Newfoundland in May.

The Isle of Birds

You can follow Jacques Cartier's journey on the maps on pp. 42-43.

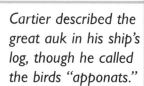

Cartier described the great auk in his ship's log, though he called the birds "apponats."

Once the ice melted and the sea cleared, Cartier headed for the northern tip of Newfoundland. He soon came upon an island that French fishermen called the "Isle of Birds." It was well named. The island was home to thousands and thousands of birds, who perched and sang on the rocky ledges of the island. Some fisherman came to the island regularly to hunt the birds for food. There were so many birds on the island that hunting them was never very difficult. Today, the island is called Funk Island.

Birds and bears

Cartier and his sailors called these birds "apponats," but they later became known as great auks. Because they were so fat, the birds became a favorite target for Cartier's hunters. He writes that on one hunt, "in less than half an hour we loaded our two **longboats** with them as if they were stones." They killed so many birds, in fact, that they couldn't eat them all. They salted some to preserve the meat, so that it could be eaten later.

Polar bears came to the islands near Newfoundland to feed on birds. Their speed in the water impressed the sailors. Cartier writes that one bear "as big as a calf and white as a swan" swam so fast that the ship could barely keep up with it.

Into the ice

Cartier's ships rounded the tip of Newfoundland and sailed into the **Strait** of Belle Isle, a narrow waterway that leads into the broad Gulf of St. Lawrence. Cartier found the strait choked with floating ice. He had to make his way carefully through the ice, taking care that the largest chunks didn't damage his wooden ships. By June, he had made his way through the ice and into the wide gulf. He was now ready to begin his search for the way to Asia.

In Cartier's words:

"[The Isle of Birds] is so very much filled with birds that they look as if they had been stowed there. Roundabout and in the air there are a hundred times as many as on the island. Some are as big as geese, and black and white, with beaks like a crow's, and they are always in the sea, without ever being able to fly ... And these birds are so fat that it is a marvelous thing."

Funk Island is still home to thousands of birds. Although the great auk became **extinct** almost 200 years ago, the island still has large numbers of such birds as puffins, gulls, and storm petrels.

Into Unknown Waters

You can follow Jacques Cartier's journey on the maps on pp. 42-43.

Cartier headed south and west into what is now called the Gulf of St. Lawrence. At the time, however, he had no way of knowing that he was at the entrance to a mighty river that could lead him deep into the interior of North America. He was now in waters that were unknown to European sailors. By June, temperatures had become so warm that ice was no longer a problem. However, fog still made navigation difficult.

Navigation

There were no maps for the waters Cartier had entered. Without maps, even the best navigational instruments were of limited use. Cartier had only a few tools to help find his way, such as the **compass,** an instrument that tells sailors which direction they're going. He also used other instruments that helped him tell the location of his ship, based upon the position of stars. These included the **cross-staff,** the **astrolabe,** and the **quadrant.**

Even with these instruments, a **navigator** like Cartier depended upon years of experience to help him find his way. Only an experienced sailor could have a sense for how fast his ship was going or the condition of the seas he was entering. Cartier used his experience to lead his ships safely for 300 miles (483 kilometers) through the fog. He reached the southwestern tip of Newfoundland on June 24.

Native Americans along the St. Lawrence River made canoes from the bark of birch trees, which were plentiful in the area.

Encountering Native Americans

Along the way, Cartier observed a group of Native Americans on the shore. He described their canoes, which they made from the bark of birch trees. The birchbark canoe was an ideal craft for river travel, because it was light but sturdy. It was so light that a single person could easily carry one on his back. Later French explorers would use the birchbark canoe for their travels.

Navigational devices like the astrolabe helped bring about the age of European exploration.

In Cartier's words:

*"These natives, men and women alike, clothe themselves in **pelts,** but the women are more wrapped in their pelts and are belted at the waist. They all paint themselves with tawny colors."*

LATITUDE AND LONGITUDE

Cartier's navigational tools helped him tell the **latitude,** or north-south position of his ships, but they were no help in finding his **longitude,** or east-west position. In fact, it wasn't until 200 years after Cartier sailed that sailors could accurately calculate their longitude at sea. In 1714, the British government offered a prize to any inventor who could come up with a device to tell sailors their longitude. In 1735, an English clockmaker named John Harrison introduced such a device. It was called the marine chronometer and it was highly accurate. Harrison was awarded a prize of 20,000 pounds, a huge fortune in those days.

New Encounters

You can follow Jacques Cartier's journey on the maps on pp. 42-43.

As Cartier sailed through the Gulf of St. Lawrence, he discovered lush islands thick with vegetation. These islands were a welcome change from the rocky shoreline of Newfoundland.

"Most excellent land"

Cartier called one of the islands "the most excellent land we have seen, for two acres of it are worth more than all the New Lands [Newfoundland]." Cartier named the island Brion Island, in honor of France's top **admiral.** There he found fields of wild oats growing so well that it looked as if a farmer had planted them. The island was also home to many different kinds of animals, including a creature unknown to the French. Cartier described the animal as something like a large ox, except with tusks like an elephant. He was describing a walrus.

In the warm and pleasant days of summer, the spirits of Cartier's men must have soared. On July 4, they reached a piece of land that marked the opening of a bay stretching to the west. Could this be the way to Asia? Cartier named it Cape Hope and sent some of his men in a **longboat** to explore it. They returned with the report that the bay was surrounded by beautiful green woods, but that it was not the desired shortcut to Asia. Cartier named it Chaleur Bay, or the Bay of Heat.

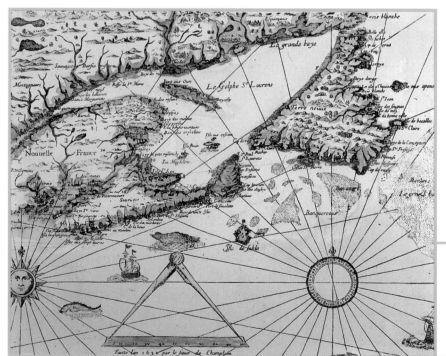

The St. Lawrence River led explorers from the Atlantic Ocean into the interior of North America.

16

Encounter with the Micmacs

Cartier and his men had spotted Native Americans on shore, but they had not yet met any of them. Once, they tried to row toward a lone person standing on the shore, but he ran away when they approached. Later, when Cartier was in Chaleur Bay, a group of Native Americans in about 50 canoes rowed out toward him. They belonged to a tribe called the Micmacs. Cartier ordered two small cannons fired over their heads, to frighten them off. The next day, the Micmacs approached the French again. This time, Cartier rowed out to meet them in a longboat. He gave their chief a red wool cap and his men offered knives and **hatchets** in exchange for animal **pelts.** Soon, hundreds of Micmacs arrived, all wanting to meet the newcomers. Cartier even managed to learn a few words in the Micmacs' language.

Cartier and his followers had never seen anything like the walrus. This engraving, made in 1560, was probably drawn by someone who had never seen a real walrus, only read descriptions of them.

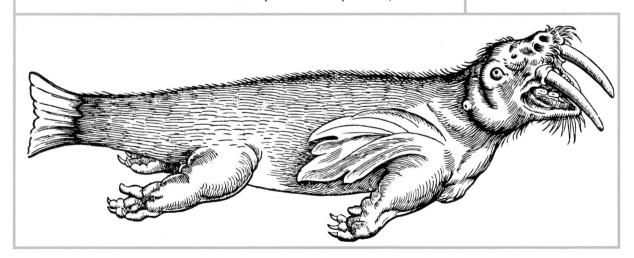

With the Iroquois

After trading with the Micmacs for a few days, Cartier decided to continue on his way. He headed north through violent storms until landing at the Gaspé **Peninsula.** There, Cartier's men met another group of Native Americans, who spoke a different language than the Micmacs. These were probably Iroquois.

Trading with the Iroquois

As he had with the Micmacs, Cartier began trading with the Iroquois. He had brought with him a supply of goods for trading, including **hatchets,** knives, beaded jewelry, and brightly colored clothing. In return, the Iroquois offered the **pelts** of animals such as the beaver. In the years to come, French and English traders in Canada would make fortunes supplying beaver skins to Europe, where they were used to make hats and other expensive goods.

Claiming the land for France

On July 24, 1534, Cartier and his men gathered for a special ceremony. On the shore of the Gaspé Peninsula, he erected a huge cross. It reached 30 feet (9 meters) into the air. On it was hung a shield engraved with a fleur-de-lis, the symbol of France.

This painting depicts Cartier planting the cross on the Gaspé Peninsula. You can see the fleur-de-lis on his flag.

Below that were the words, "Long live the king of France." By planting the cross, Cartier was claiming possession of the land for France. It didn't matter to him that the Native Americans had already lived there for hundreds of years.

Then he began making plans for his return voyage. He told the Iroquois leader that he wanted the chief's two sons to return to France with him. Cartier knew that bringing these Native Americans home would impress his king. He also wanted the boys—named Domagaia and Taignoagny—to learn French so that they could serve as interpreters on his next exploration. The chief was reluctant, but eventually he agreed to let his sons go.

In Cartier's words:

"[The Iroquois] have no other lodging but their canoes which they turn up and sleep under on the ground. They eat their meat nearly raw after they have warmed it slightly on the coals ... They have their heads shaved all around, except for a bit on the top of the head which they leave long like a horse's tail and which they tie and knot on their heads like leather."

THE IROQUOIS

The Iroquois were a **confederacy** of several tribes. Each was pledged to help defend the others against common enemies. They also spoke related languages. Iroquois tribes included the Mohawks, Oneidas, Onondagas, Cayugas, and Senecas. Their territory stretched from the Atlantic coast to the Great Lakes region.

This illustration shows Europeans trading with Native Americans for valuable furs. The furs could be sold for high prices in Europe.

A Second Voyage

You can follow Jacques Cartier's journey on the maps on pp. 42-43.

Cartier could have explored further, but he decided to return home. On July 25th, Cartier departed the mainland of North America with Domagaia and Taignoagny aboard. Cartier began heading back toward the Atlantic Ocean, pausing to explore the waters around present-day Anticosti Island. The passage there is now named for Cartier. For some reason, Cartier never stopped to explore the St. Lawrence River itself, though he sailed past the entrance to it. That would have to wait for future explorations.

Returning home

Instead, Cartier set his two ships on a course for France. They made the long ocean crossing back to Europe without difficulty, and by September 5 they were within sight of home. Cartier had made it back to St. Malo without losing a single member of his crew. He had not found a shortcut to Asia, nor were his ships full of gold. Still, he wanted to continue to explore some of the areas he had been unable to reach. King Francis I agreed. On October 31, Cartier received permission from the King to return to North America. The king even called Cartier "France's pilot of the western sea."

Cartier waited until his second voyage to sail down the St. Lawrence River.

The "Great Commission"

Cartier's assignment for the second voyage was to explore the waters beyond Anticosti Island. The king hoped that Cartier might find a route to China there. He also had a second task for Cartier. This time, Cartier was to teach the Native Americans he met the Catholic religion. This part of Cartier's assignment was called the "Great Commission."

Cartier was given command of three ships: The *Grande Hermine*, the *Petite Hermine* and the *Emerillon*. The largest was the *Grande Hermine*, which could carry 120 tons and could fire 12 cannons. The ships would be sailed by a crew of 112 men. This was to be a larger and more ambitious voyage than Cartier's first. Also on board would be Domagaia and Taignoagny.

Beginning with Cartier's second voyage, the French worked to **convert** Native Americans to Catholicism.

On May 16, 1535, Cartier and his crew attended services at the cathedral in St. Malo. Three days later, they set out across the Atlantic.

THE GRANDE HERMINE

Cartier's flagship was called the *Grande Hermine*. It was a galleon, a type of large warship with two decks and three masts. Galleons were large enough to carry huge cargoes. In fact, Spanish galleons transported gold and other treasures from the Americas to Europe. The *Grande Hermine* was twice the size of the ships Cartier commanded in his first voyage to North America. Cartier probably hoped that he too would have a cargo of treasure to transport back to Europe.

The Journey to Stadacona

YOU CAN FOLLOW JACQUES CARTIER'S JOURNEY ON THE MAPS ON PP. 42-43.

By early August, Cartier had made it across the Atlantic Ocean and back to Anticosti Island. This was as far as he had explored on his first visit. Now he was determined to push beyond the island, into the interior of the country.

Exploring the St. Lawrence

Luckily for Cartier, he had the two Native American brothers, Domagaia and Taignoagny, to help guide him. As he sailed into the broad expanse of water beyond Anticosti Island, Cartier assumed he was sailing on a great sea. However, his Native American guides told him that he was on a huge river. The river would one day be called the St. Lawrence.

Cartier stopped to map the mouth of this great river. He found that its mouth—the place where the river empties into the sea—was more than 80 miles (130 kilometers) wide from north to south. He also spotted more whales than he had ever seen before. The shores of the river were rich with plant and animal life, but for hundreds of miles, Cartier did not meet a single person. Finally, near the spot where another river empties into the St. Lawrence, the Frenchmen met a group of Native Americans. With Domagaia and Taignoagny acting as translators, they came aboard one of the ships for a short visit.

Québec takes its name from a Native American word meaning "place where the river narrows."

This painting shows Cartier sailing down the St. Lawrence River. After crossing the Atlantic Ocean, his crew must have enjoyed seeing the amazing scenery along the river.

Meeting with Donnacona

Further upriver, the Frenchmen came to a Native American village called Stadacona. The village was alongside the St. Lawrence at a place where the river narrows. The French would later build a city they named Québec at the same site. Cartier met there with Donnacona, the leader of all the villages in the area. He learned that the Native Americans called the region Canada, meaning "town" or "village." He learned that there was another Native American village called Hochelaga, further up the river. He also learned that to the north was a land called Saguenay, which the Native Americans said was rich in valuable minerals. However, the Native Americans tried to scare Cartier away from these places. They even dressed as evil spirits who had come to warn Cartier of the dangers ahead. But none of their efforts succeeded. Cartier was determined to see these places for himself.

NATURAL RICHES

Cartier came to Canada looking for gold. Instead, he found other kinds of riches, like the abundant plant and animal life of Canada. Most valuable of all was the beaver, whose skins were highly prized by Native Americans and later by Europeans as well. The forests of Canada made an ideal home for beavers. The animals grew thick, glossy coats to survive cold Canadian winters. In the 1600s, hats and other garments made from beaver fur became very fashionable in Europe.

Visiting Hochelaga

You can follow Jacques Cartier's journey on the maps on pp. 42-43.

On September 19, 1535, Cartier headed up the St. Lawrence River, bound for the village of Hochelaga. Knowing that his crew would need shelter for the coming winter, he left some of his men behind to build a fort near the Native American village at Stadacona. For eleven days, Cartier sailed up the river, past trees blazing with autumn color. On October 1, he reached the village of Hochelaga.

In the village

The village was surrounded by a **palisade,** a kind of wood enclosure used for defense. More than 1,000 Native Americans rushed out of the village to greet Cartier. When he went ashore, their leaders presented him with gifts of fish and cornbread and guided him into the village. Cartier later described the Native American houses: "There are about 50 houses in the village. Each of these is about 50 or more paces long and 12 or 15 paces wide, built entirely of wood covered and trimmed with large pieces of bark and strippings from the trees..." Each house was divided into several large rooms and sheltered several families.

Visitors to Montréal can still climb Mount Royal, just as Cartier did, and get a beautiful view of the city.

The Native Americans prepared a celebration for Cartier. He and his men were asked to sit on mats in the square at the center of the village. The village's elderly chief was carried to meet Cartier. He took the crown off his own head and presented it to Cartier.

This illustration show Iroquois houses of the type Cartier found at Hochelaga.

Climbing *Mont Réal*

For five days, Cartier and his men stayed with the Native Americans. As Cartier was preparing to leave, he decided to climb the tall mountain that towered over the village. Cartier named the mountain *Mont Réal,* or Mount Royal. The city of Montréal later took its name from the mountain. Native American guides led him to the top, from where he could see far in all directions. His eyes followed the St. Lawrence far off into the west. However, **rapids** blocked the way west. Large ships could not hope to get past the rapids, and this meant that the St. Lawrence River was definitely not the desired passage to Asia. With winter approaching, Cartier knew it was time to return to Stadacona and his new fort.

In Cartier's words:

"Along both shores, we saw the most excellent and beautiful land that can be seen, smooth as a pond and covered with the finest trees in the world, and along the River were so many vines laden with grapes that they seemed to have been planted by human hands."

Winter Quarters

YOU CAN FOLLOW JACQUES CARTIER'S JOURNEY ON THE MAPS ON PP. 42-43.

By October, cold winds were already blowing out of the north. Cartier and the other Frenchmen were about to experience their first winter in North America. On October 11, they arrived at the new fort that some of the men had built near Stadacona. Its outside wall was made of logs sharpened and driven into the earth. Inside were huts in which the men could take shelter from the cold. Cannons were mounted high on the walls to fire at attackers. Nearby, Cartier's ships were anchored in the river.

Cartier tried to gather information from Donnacona about the land surrounding Stadacona. He was especially curious about the land the Native Americans called Saguenay. They told Cartier that he could find silver, copper, and other precious metals in Saguenay.

Fear of a Native American attack

However, relations between the Frenchmen and the Native Americans soon took a turn for the worse. Some of the Native Americans began to be dissatisfied with the trinkets the French

Cartier's huge ships must have impressed the Native Americans as they sailed into harbor near Stadacona.

The snow and icy cold of Canadian winter surprised Cartier's crew.

offered for trade. Domagaia and Taignoagny had spent a winter in France and told their own people that the French owned much more valuable items than cheap whistles or wool hats.

Cartier began to fear a Native American attack. He ordered the walls of the fort to be strengthened and a ditch to be dug around the outside. He had his men build a new gate with a **drawbridge.** He ordered 50 men to keep guard at night.

However, it was the harsh cold and the brutal living conditions that did the most damage to the French. Before the winter was over, many of the French would fall victim to a disease they did not know how to cure.

UNPREPARED FOR WINTER

Cartier and his crew were the first Frenchmen to spend a winter in the far north of North America. Because Québec is farther south than Paris, they expected a mild winter, much like the weather they were used to in France. They had no idea how cold and snowy it could get. Cartier wrote that from the middle of November until the middle of April, the snow was always about 4 feet (1.2 meters) deep.

A Deadly Disease

You can follow Jacques Cartier's journey on the maps on pp. 42-43.

The winter proved to be colder and snowier than anything they had experienced in France. By November, the French ships were stuck in the river, which had frozen solid. Snow began to pile high against the walls of the fort. The food supply dwindled until they were living on dried corn and salted meat. They had no fresh fruits or vegetables.

Scurvy

Soon, many of Cartier's men began to weaken and grow ill. They developed sores on their bodies, and their arms and legs began to swell. Their gums bled and their teeth became loose. Of the 110 men in Cartier's company, 100 became ill. Eight of them died. Worst of all, Cartier and his men had no idea what to do about the disease.

Today we know that Cartier's men were suffering from scurvy. Scurvy is a disorder caused by a lack of vitamin C. Vitamin C is found in many fruits and vegetables, such as oranges, limes, tomatoes, and green peppers. However, Cartier's men had no way of getting fresh fruits or vegetables in the cold of the Canadian winter.

Chief Donnacona gave Cartier a warm welcome when they first met. Their relationship would not always be so friendly.

SCURVY

For centuries, sailors suffered from scurvy because they couldn't stock fresh fruits on long voyages. In 1747, a Scottish doctor named James Lind noticed that limes and oranges helped prevent scurvy. In 1795, the British Navy began feeding its sailors regular doses of lime juice. Because of this, they were often called "limeys."

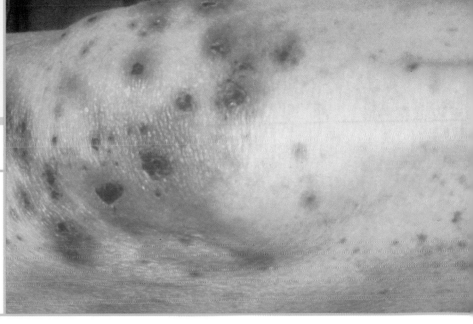

This person is suffering from one of the stages of scurvy, in which bleeding sores develop on the arms and legs. It can be cured by taking vitamin C.

They were rescued by a cure that the Native Americans had discovered. The Iroquois taught the French to brew a kind of tea made from the bark and needles of a tree they called the *annedda*. Cartier had all his sick men drink the tea, and the cure worked so well that all of them were cured in just over a week. He wrote that all the doctors of France could not have worked such a miraculous cure.

Capturing Donnacona

With the aid of the Native Americans, the Frenchmen made it through the terrible winter. However, when spring came, Cartier betrayed them. He captured their chief, Donnacona, so that the chief could return to France with him. He wanted King Francis to hear about the riches of Saguenay from the chief himself. Donnacona's people were angry, but Cartier promised to return the chief within a year.

Delays and Deaths

You can follow Jacques Cartier's journey on the maps on pp. 42-43.

In May of 1536, a weary Cartier headed back for France, with his ten Iroquois captives aboard. Disease had thinned the ranks of his expedition, so that he could sail only two ships home. He left the third behind on the St. Lawrence River. On the way home, he explored a new route, along the southern coast of Newfoundland. His two ships arrived in St. Malo on July 6.

This illustration shows privateers capturing an enemy ship.

War with Spain

Cartier was eager to arrange a meeting with King Francis, so that he could meet Donnacona and hear about the land on the other side of the ocean. The king had more pressing concerns, however. Not long after Cartier's return, Spain invaded France, setting off a war between the two countries. Now the king was more interested in winning the war with his European neighbor than he was in exploring North America.

PRIVATEERS

Privateers were owners or captains of ships who had permission from their government to attack and raid ships of enemy nations. (Their ships were called privateers, too.) Privateers kept any loot they captured. The governments that hired privateers were able to attack enemy nations without risking the ships or men of the official navy. By the 1800s, most nations considered privateering to be against the rules of war.

Cartier did his part to help. He took the *Grande Hermine* into the Atlantic Ocean and began raiding Spanish and Portuguese ships as a privateer. Whatever money, weapons, or other treasures Cartier captured, he contributed to the French war effort. The war lasted until 1538, when the two countries signed the Treaty of Nice, named for the French city where it was signed.

Plans for a colony

As soon as the war ended, Cartier began asking the king for permission to return to North America. He asked for command of a fleet of 6 ships, with nearly 300 people on board. There would be not only sailors, but also carpenters, mechanics, **masons, blacksmiths,** priests, and doctors on board. This time, Cartier wanted not only to explore, but also to establish a French **colony** in North America. Cartier's colonists would bring seeds, farm animals, tools, farming equipment, and everything else they would need to build a thriving French village in the woods of Canada.

The king agreed to send Cartier on a third voyage. However, the king's decision came too late for Cartier's Iroquois captives. For several years they had lived in France, waiting for the chance to return to their homeland. Unused to the strange surroundings, they grew ill one by one and died in France.

In the words of King Francis I:

"We send our dear and well-beloved Jacques Cartier, who has discovered great tracts of the countries of Canada and Hochelaga ... to the said countries of Canada and Hochelaga, and as far as the land of Saguenay, should he be able to penetrate thither."

War between France and Spain delayed Cartier's third voyage.

The Colonial Expedition

You can follow Jacques Cartier's journey on the maps on pp. 42-43.

Cartier's third voyage to North America would be the largest and most ambitious yet. However, he would not be in command of the expedition. King Francis had appointed a French **nobleman** named Jean-François de La Rocque, **Sieur** de Roberval, to lead the effort to establish a French **colony** in Canada. He would have the title of governor of the colony. Cartier was given the lesser title of captain-general. Roberval had no experience as a sea captain, nor had he ever tried to start an overseas colony. He was given command over Cartier for one reason: because he was a nobleman and Cartier was not.

Roberval's troubles

Roberval's plan was to divide the land along the St. Lawrence River into plots. He would sell these to French farmers, who would have to give some of the profits they earned by farming back to Roberval. Of course, the Native Americans who already lived on the land were not consulted about any of this.

Cartier sailed the Grande Hermine *and the* Émérillon *on his third voyage, as well as three other ships.*

Roberval's plan was a failure from the start. He had trouble raising money to pay for supplies for the trip. He also couldn't persuade enough French families to move to a strange land across the sea and start a new life. Instead, he stocked the expedition with people who had been serving sentences in France's prisons. While Roberval was trying to solve all his problems, Cartier waited in St. Malo for the go-ahead to sail for Canada.

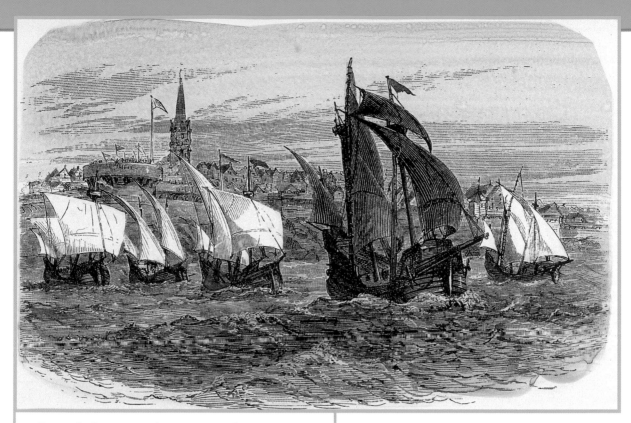

Cartier's fleet must have received an impressive send-off as they sailed from St. Malo.

Return to Stadacona

Finally, Cartier could wait no longer. On May 23, 1541, he set off across the Atlantic. It would be another year before Roberval followed. Cartier's ocean crossing was a difficult one. Severe storms rocked his five ships so badly that they became separated from each other. Many of the farm animals on board nearly died. It was three months before Cartier's ships reunited on the St. Lawrence River.

One of Cartier's first tasks was meeting with the Native Americans of Stadacona. Five years earlier, he had left with ten of their people, promising to return within a year. When the new chief, named Agona, asked where Donnacona and the others were, Cartier lied. He told Agona that most of the Native Americans had married and were living in France "like lords." However, he did admit that Donnacona had died in France. Cartier's lies would soon come back to haunt him, as word spread among the Native Americans that he could not be trusted.

The Colony at Charlesbourg Royal

YOU CAN FOLLOW JACQUES CARTIER'S JOURNEY ON THE MAPS ON PP. 42-43.

Cartier chose a spot at the junction of the St. Lawrence and Cap Rouge rivers for the new **colony.** The soil there appeared to be ideal for farming, and the surrounding woods would supply lumber for the colony. He anchored his ships there and sent his men ashore to begin preparing the land.

Building a settlement

He ordered his builders to build two structures. One was located on top of a steep **bluff,** the other at the foot of the same bluff. Each had a tall observation tower. Farmers set to work clearing the fields near the buildings. They cut down trees and removed large boulders, then planted seeds for wheat and vegetables. The soil proved to be so fertile that the seeds began sending up tender shoots within days. Cartier named the little settlement Charlesbourg Royal, after France's Prince Charles.

DANGEROUS WATERS

Rapids in the St. Lawrence River blocked Cartier's way west. If Cartier had gone a little way past the rapids, he would have discovered a large island in the St. Lawrence River. Historians know that Cartier didn't travel that far, because none of the maps based on Cartier's explorations show the island.

The rapids in the St. Lawrence River near Hochelaga blocked large ships and boats from traveling farther inland.

This photo shows the junction of the Cap Rouge and St. Lawrence rivers, where Cartier built a French settlement.

At the site of the new settlement, Cartier made a discovery that seemed to make all the danger and hardship of exploration worthwhile. He found nuggets of stone in the riverbed—nuggets that he believed were gold. On a nearby mountain, he found what he was sure were diamonds. He had heard tales of the riches of Saguenay, but he seemed to be finding treasure already.

In search of Saguenay

With work proceeding on the settlement, Cartier prepared to sail inland once more. He hoped to learn more about Saguenay, the land that Donnacona and others had told him about years earlier. On September 17, he set off in two **longboats.** His goal was to explore near the rapids in the St. Lawrence River that blocked the way west. He would have to find a way around the rapids, if he was to make it to Saguenay.

Getting around the rapids was no easy matter, however. His men were able to get past one set of rapids, but the next set proved too dangerous. The swift current and hidden boulders would have dashed the French boats to pieces. Even worse, winter was once again approaching. Cartier had learned by bitter experience how deadly the northern winters could be. He raced back to the shelter of Charlesbourg Royal.

Abandoning the Colony

YOU CAN FOLLOW JACQUES CARTIER'S JOURNEY ON THE MAPS ON PP. 42-43.

Cartier had another reason for wanting to reach the safety of his new fort. More and more he began to suspect that the Native Americans along the St. Lawrence River no longer welcomed him. On his way back to Charlesbourg Royal, word came to him that the Native Americans were gathering for an attack on the French. When he reached Charlesbourg Royal that fall, he sent scouts toward the village of Stadacona. They returned to tell Cartier that many Native Americans had indeed gathered there, perhaps for an attack.

A winter of hardship

Concerned about the possibility of an attack, Cartier ordered the fort at Charlesbourg Royal to be strengthened. Just as he had done six year earlier, Cartier would have to wait out a cold Canadian winter in a newly-built fort. However, this time he would not be able to turn to his Native American neighbors for help. Once again, the waters of the rivers froze, and the bitter winds cut through the walls of the fort. When the weather allowed it, the Iroquois launched raids on the French. They attacked them anytime they dared to venture outside the fort.

Cartier met Roberval in the harbor of St. John's, Newfoundland, a year after he left St. Malo.

Cartier found only fool's gold in Canada, not the real thing.

Hurrying home

In the spring of 1542, Cartier forgot all about his plan to find Saguenay. Instead, in early June, he pointed his ships toward the Atlantic Ocean and headed towards home. Defeated and discouraged, he sailed down the St. Lawrence toward Newfoundland. There, he happened to meet Roberval, whose ships were finally arriving in Canada after a delay of more than a year. Of course, Roberval was more than a little surprised to see Cartier already heading home. However, Roberval had not yet had to deal with deadly cold and hostile Iroquois.

Roberval ordered Cartier to return to Charlesbourg Royal, but Cartier refused. He knew his men had experienced enough hardship. Instead, he slipped away into the Atlantic Ocean, bound for France. Cartier had very little to show for his year in Canada, except some stones that might be gold or diamonds. When he arrived in France in October 1542, Cartier was eager to have the stones examined by experts. However, what Cartier hoped were diamonds turned out be pieces of less valuable quartz. And what he hoped was gold was a mineral called pyrite that only looked like gold. Some people called it "fool's gold."

Cartier's Last Years

Even after Cartier abandoned him in Newfoundland, Roberval was not ready to give up on the **colony** on the banks of the St. Lawrence River. He sailed up the river and built a new, larger fort at the site of Cartier's fort. He renamed the settlement France-Roy.

Roberval in Canada

Roberval's colonists—including the first French women to live in North America—spent a miserable winter there, just as Cartier's had. Diseases killed some of them. The others had to make do with so little food that the entire colony nearly starved to death. Nor were Roberval's efforts at exploration successful. He was unable to proceed any further than Cartier had. He did not find Saguenay, nor did he find the riches that Donnacona had promised. When the spring thaw came, Roberval too gave up and returned to France.

Some historians believe that Cartier may have returned to Canada once more, to rescue Roberval and his colonists. However, there are no written records of such a rescue mission. Roberval did return to France on his own, where he died in 1561.

*Maps of Cartier's voyages were widely published and aided other **navigators** for hundreds of years.*

The aging explorer

Cartier lived a quiet, prosperous life at his estate near St. Malo. We know very little for certain about Cartier's final years, except that he remained one of the most respected citizens of St. Malo. In the church records there, he is listed again and again as godfather to newborn babies at their **baptism** in the Catholic Church. In Cartier's time, this was an honor reserved for people of great achievement or importance.

In his last years, Cartier's home was a popular destination for mapmakers and others curious about the land across the ocean. Cartier's maps, journals, and logbooks remained the only information available to Europeans about Canada for the next 50 years. Only in the 1600s would French explorers return to Canada to build upon his accomplishment. Cartier died on September 1, 1557. Unlike so many other explorers of his day, he died not violently in a strange land, but peacefully in his hometown.

Cartier's Legacy

While Cartier was beginning his explorations of the St. Lawrence River, Spain's Francisco Pizarro was conquering Peru in South America. There, Pizarro found temples filled with gold and other treasures that would help make Spain rich.

Compared to the treasure Pizarro found, Cartier's explorations produced unimpressive results. Even the gold Cartier thought he had found turned out not to be gold at all. Not surprisingly, France's kings quickly lost interest in funding more explorations of Canada. After Cartier returned from his failed effort to start a **colony** in Canada, no French explorer returned there for more than 60 years.

However, there were riches other than gold to be found in Canada. These included the forests of tall trees, the schools of fish swimming off Canada's coast, and the plentiful moose, elk, and beavers. Europeans who came after Cartier would make fortunes from the natural bounty of Canada. They would also deplete the supply of those natural riches. For example, French traders in the 1600s earned profits by trading with Native Americans for beaver **pelts** that were in high demand in Europe.

Wealthy people there wanted the pelts for use in fashionable hats and coats. Before long, trappers trapped so many beavers that the animals became hard to find. The trappers had to move west to find more.

Samuel de Champlain, the "father of New France," explored New England and the St. Lawrence River.

Cartier and the French also changed the lives of Native Americans. Some tribes were completely wiped out by the diseases Europeans brought with them. Others were pushed out of their homelands, or involved in French wars. After Cartier, French **missionaries** converted many Native Americans to Christianity. Just as Cartier did, later explorers lied to Native Americans and attacked them.

The natural riches of Canada encouraged exploration after Cartier.

It wasn't until 1608 that a French explorer named Samuel de Champlain made his way down the St. Lawrence River. He founded the first permanent French settlement in Canada, the city of Québec. He built it not far from the site of Cartier's failed colony, 60 years earlier.

Champlain became known as the "father of New France," or Canada. However, 60 years before Champlain, Cartier had made the first French claims to the area. His explorations paved the way for Champlain and others to follow. Cartier had not found the riches he hoped to find in Canada, nor did he find the sea route to Asia. His attempt at colonizing Canada failed, as well. However, his discovery of the St. Lawrence River and his explorations deep into the interior of Canada earned him a place among history's great explorers.

DISAPPEARING IROQUOIS

When Champlain arrived in the St. Lawrence River region, he did not find the Iroquois villages there that Cartier had visited 60 years before. The Iroquois had abandoned the area, possibly driven out by other Indians. In the 1600s, the Iroquois became the most feared group of Indians in what is now the northeast United States. They controlled land stretching from present-day Maine to present day Illinois.

Maps of Cartier's Expeditions

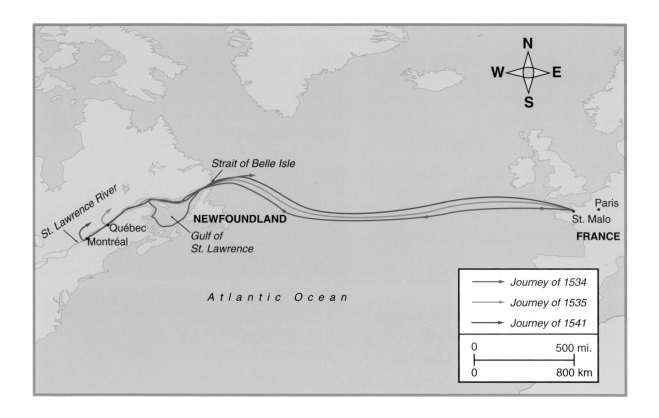

Jacques Cartier probably followed a similar route across the Atlantic Ocean on each of his three voyages, based on the winds and ocean currents that were the most favorable. On his first trip to North America, he explored the islands and coasts of eastern Canada. It was not until his second and third voyages that he explored deep into the interior of the country, following the St. Lawrence River as far as the site of present-day Montréal.

You can see an overview of Cartier's three voyages in the map above. The map at the top of page 43 shows a close-up of his explorations around Newfoundland and the Gulf of St. Lawrence in 1534. The bottom map shows a closer view of his voyages down the St. Lawrence River in 1535 and 1541.

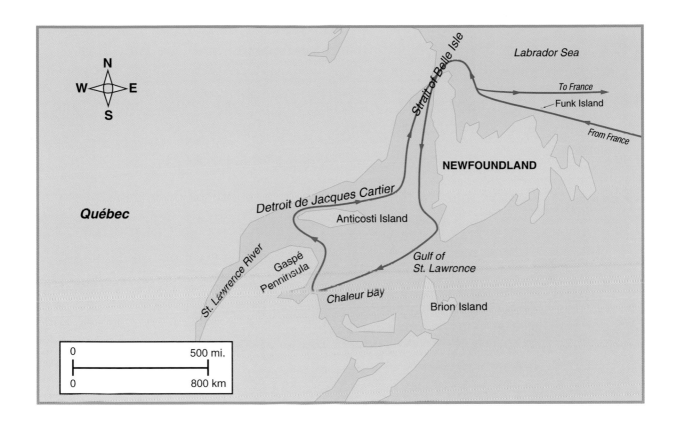

Labrador Sea

To France

Funk Island

From France

Strait of Belle Isle

NEWFOUNDLAND

Detroit de Jacques Cartier

Anticosti Island

Québec

St. Lawrence River

Gaspé Pennifsula

Gulf of St. Lawrence

Chaleur Bay

Brion Island

N
W E
S

| 0 | 500 mi. |
| 0 | 800 km |

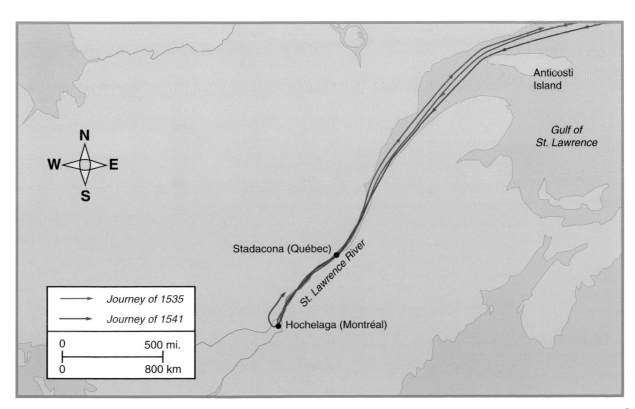

Anticosti Island

Gulf of St. Lawrence

Stadacona (Québec)

St. Lawrence River

Hochelaga (Montréal)

N
W E
S

Journey of 1535
Journey of 1541

| 0 | 500 mi. |
| 0 | 800 km |

Timeline

1491	Jacques Cartier is born in St. Malo, France.
1492	Christopher Columbus sails for Asia and finds the Americas instead.
1497	John Cabot is sent by the English to explore Newfoundland and discovers the Grand Banks.
1515	Francis I becomes king of France at the age of 21.
1519	Cartier marries the daughter of a local official in St. Malo.
1522	The voyage led by Ferdinand Magellan completes its journey around the world.
1524	Giovanni da Verrazano explores the Atlantic coast of North America, looking for the **Northwest Passage.**
1532	Francisco Pizarro conquers the Incas, bringing great wealth to Spain.
1533	King Francis I orders Cartier to explore the seas beyond Newfoundland.
1534	Cartier departs on his first voyage to North America (April 20). He claims Canada for France (July 24). He returns to France (September 5). He receives orders to make a second voyage to North America (October 31).
1535	Cartier begins his second voyage (May 16). He arrives at Hochelega (October 1). He arrives at the new fort near Stadacona to spend the winter (October 11).
1536	Cartier returns to France after a deadly winter in Canada.
1536-38	War between Spain and France.
1541	Cartier departs from St. Malo on his third voyage on May 23.
1542	Cartier arrives home from last voyage in October. On the way, his ships meet up with Roberval's expedition.

1543	Roberval gives up on the colony and returns to France.
1547	Francis I of France dies. His son, Henry II, becomes king.
1557	Jacques Cartier dies on September 1 at his home in St. Malo.
1561	Roberval dies in France.
1567	Samuel de Champlain is born.
1608	Champlain establishes a settlement at Québec.
1747	James Lind discovers that oranges and limes help to prevent scurvy.
1906	Norwegian explorer Roald Amundsen becomes the first person to sail the Northwest Passage.

More Books to Read

Champion, Neil. *John Cabot.* Chicago: Heinemann Library, 2001.

Harmon, Daniel E. *Jacques Cartier and the Exploration of Canada.* Broomall, Penn.: Chelsea House, 2001.

Sonneborn, Liz. *Samuel de Champlain.* Danbury, Conn.: Franklin Watts, 2001.

Glossary

admiral high-ranking position in a navy

astrolabe instrument that helps sailors navigate by the position of the sun and the stars

baptism ceremony in which a person is dunked in water or has water sprinkled on his or her head, as part of the process of joining a Christian church

blacksmith person who works with iron, especially to make horseshoes

bluff high, steep cliff or bank

compass instrument that indicates direction. It consists of a magnetic needle that turns to always point north.

colony group of people sent out by a state or country to settle a new territory

confederacy union of peoples, groups, or states for a certain purpose

convert to persuade someone to change their religious beliefs, either by choice or force

cross-staff instrument used in the 1400s and 1500s to navigate by the position of the sun and stars

drawbridge bridge that can be pulled or drawn up to prevent people from crossing it

empire group of countries or territories under the control of one government or ruler

extinct having died out completely, as a species

flagship most important ship in a fleet, on which the commander of the fleet travels

hammock hanging bed made of canvas and rope

hatchet small ax with a short handle

latitude distance north or south of the Equator

longboat small boat, similar to a modern-day lifeboat, carried on a larger ship. They were usually used to ferry crew to shore and to explore shallow waters.

longitude distance east or west of the "prime meridian" line, which runs through Greenwich, England

maggot insect, especially a fly, in an early stage, when it looks like a worm

mast tall pole set on the deck of a ship, on which sails are hung

mason person who builds things with bricks or stones

missionary someone sent out by a church to spread its religion in a foreign country

navigator someone who is trained to figure the path of a ship

nobleman person of high birth or rank

Northwest Passage sea route from Europe to Asia that runs north of North America. Explorers tried for centuries to find it.

palisade fence made of stakes set in the ground, used for protection or defense

pelt skin of an animal, including the fur

peninsula long piece of land almost completely surrounded by water

quadrant instrument used to navigate by the position of the sun and stars

rapid a part of a river where the current moves very swiftly, making it difficult to navigate

Sieur title meaning "Gentleman," used by some noblemen in France

strait narrow body of water that connects two larger ones

Index